NORTH EAST BUSES TODAY

PETER TUCKER

AMBERLEY

*The book is dedicated to the late Peter McPartland, Paul McPartland and
Revd Gerald Flood of Biggin Hill.*

Front Cover: Stagecoach No. 28022 at Aldenham Road, Gilley Law on 16 March 2020.

Back Cover: Seaton Carew on 25 June 2020, with Stagecoach No. 36083 nearest to the camera.

First published 2022

Amberley Publishing
The Hill, Stroud
Gloucestershire, GL5 4EP

www.amberley-books.com

Copyright © Peter Tucker, 2022

The right of Peter Tucker to be identified as
the Author of this work has been asserted in
accordance with the Copyrights, Designs and
Patents Act 1988.

ISBN 978 1 3981 0606 2 (print)
ISBN 978 1 3981 0607 9 (ebook)

British Library Cataloguing in Publication Data.
A catalogue record for this book is available from
the British Library.

Origination by Amberley Publishing.
Printed in the UK.

Introduction

In my last publication, *Urban Buses in Northern England*, I wrote: 'I very rarely photograph buses today.' That was in 2019, when my interest in the contemporary bus scene had waned. I went on to write: 'the modern bus scene is, in my opinion, less interesting. Perhaps I will change my mind when I look at today's bus scene with the benefit of hindsight, etc.'

Sometime after I had finished the book, I began to take more notice of the current transport scene. I read reports about independent operators going into administration, councils cutting subsidies and the introduction of hybrid buses. I paid more than a cursory glance at the buses being used; I liked the Mercedes-Benz Citaro but thought the Plaxton Primo was plain ugly. The rare Primo resembles one of Cleveland Transits shortened Bedford YRQs – the rear looks uncomfortably short, docked like a puppy's tail. I was intrigued by the marketing techniques used by Go North East, plus the various schemes operators used to entice customers, such as contactless payment and Wi-Fi. Maybe, I thought, the bus industry was still interesting after all.

North East Buses Today is a kind of direct sequel to *North East Buses in the 1990s*. Much has changed. While the often chaotic effects of the 1985 Transport Act were still being felt in the early 1990s, today the picture is one of corporate dominance and relative tranquillity. No longer do various companies chase a finite number of passengers and clog the streets with ageing buses, belching out toxic fumes – who can forget Darlington, Liverpool, Manchester and Sheffield after deregulation? The early days of deregulation were marked by wasteful competition plus a lack of investment in new products. The industry was saturated with used stock, such as Greater Manchester's 'Standards' and minibuses. Operators had little need for expensive Leyland Olympians and MCW Metrobuses. For various reasons Bedford, Duple, Eastern Coach Works and Roe went out of business after deregulation. Leyland Bus was absorbed into Volvo, MCW ceased production and Optare, somewhat unexpectedly, rose from the ashes of Roe at Leeds. Dennis surprised everyone by going from strength to strength, helped by the runaway success of the Dart in the 1990s. The Dart was the right product at the right time and proved effective against Volvo's B6.

Today, each of the North East's big three – Arriva, Go North East and Stagecoach – have a peaceful co-existence. There is, to use an old diplomatic expression, a 'balance of power'. Routes are carefully delineated and marketed, the unprofitable operations either hived off to independents or council tender or axed altogether. In essence, the North East PSV scene is dominated by the big three – First Group has no presence in the North East.

Arriva has a wide operating area, having effectively reconstituted the former United Automobile Services' territory north of the Tees. United Automobile Services was founded in 1912 at England's most easterly point: Lowestoft in Suffolk. The company also had a base at Bishop Auckland, a distance of approximately 255 miles. Before long United were operating across most of Eastern England, taking in places as diverse as Bungay, Cromer, East Dereham, and Mundersley. United also constructed their own buses at both Bishop Auckland and Lowestoft (1920). The Lowestoft works became Eastern Coach Works in 1936. Until relatively recently, Eastern Coach Works bodies were the dominant body choice for United and most other former NBC companies. ECW, as it was frequently abbreviated, sadly closed in 1987 as a result of rationalisation at Leyland.

The entire history of United is extremely complex so a brief summary will suffice for here. In the 1920s, United expanded into North Yorkshire, Northumberland, Lincolnshire and Norfolk. United's head office was not originally in Darlington but Lowestoft. In 1926, the head office moved from Lowestoft to York, before finally settling in Darlington in 1932. In 1929 control of the company passed to Tilling and the North Eastern Railway. The East Anglian division became the much loved Eastern Counties in 1931 with a territory eventually covering Cambridgeshire, Norfolk, Suffolk and the Soke of Peterborough (Peterborough Electric Traction). Other services would penetrate Essex, Northamptonshire and London. The head office was at Thorpe Road, Norwich, while the now demolished Surrey Street bus station and depot would provide generations of transport enthusiasts with hours of joy. The Lincolnshire Road Car Company inherited United's services in what is historically England's second largest county: Lincoln.

United was nationalised in 1948 and placed under the control of the British Transport Commission. On 1 January 1963, control passed to the Transport Holding Company. In 1969, United became a member of the National Bus Company (NBC) and promptly lost its lucrative Carlisle services to Ribble. Fleet livery was, of course, NBC poppy red, although buses operating around Tyne and Wear later adopted PTE yellow.

United's operating area was quite fascinating, embracing heavily populated conurbations, bracing seaside resorts, market towns and often spectacular rural areas. There were services to such far-flung places as Duddo, Filey, Gunnerside, Holy Island, Keld, Kelso, Kirk Yetholm (Roxburghshire), Middleton-in-Teesdale and Muker. Bus services reached cities as far apart as Carlisle, Edinburgh, Leeds, Ripon, Sunderland and York. There were also the bread and butter services in places as diverse as Allenheads, Brotton, Cambois, Coldstream, Esh Winning, Gosforth, Helmsley, Leyburn, Middlesbrough, Pickering, Peterlee, Shiremoor, Scarborough, Thirsk, Throckley and Whitley Bay, etc.

United's next major upheaval was at deregulation in 1986. The Transport Act 1985 privatised the National Bus Company. The Secretary of State Nicholas Ridley deemed Crosville, London Country, Ribble and United as too large to be sold as individual units. United was to be split up; luckily her neighbour Northern General was spared dismemberment. Crosville was divided between its Welsh and English operations. Ribble lost its Cumbrian services to an enlarged Cumberland Motor Services (making the new title a misnomer in Ambleside, Barrow, Kendal and Sedbergh). Ribble's Merseyside services went to a resurrected North Western at Bootle.

Northumbria Motor Services was formed in 1986 to take over United's services in Newcastle, North Tyneside and Northumberland. Painted in a then controversial white, red and grey, they were hard to mistake for anything else at the time. Northumbria's colour scheme was certainly advanced for the time. The radical application of bus liveries had not yet become as common place as today, although Badgerline (Bristol), Yorkshire Rider and certainly North Western could give Northumbria a run for their money. Northumbria was owned by Proudmutual and later by British Bus. According to the 1990 edition of *Bus Handbook North East England*, depots were located at Alnwick, Ashington, Berwick-upon-Tweed, Blyth, Hexham, Morpeth, Newcastle (Gallowgate and Jesmond) and Whitley Bay. Northumbria maintained outstations at Allenheads, Rothbury, Seahouses and Wooler. Northumbria's fleet consisted of the usual stock of Leopards, LHs, Nationals, Olympians and VRs inherited from United. There was also interesting acquisitions from Greater Manchester in the form of eight Fleetlines of 1976–77 vintage, plus several Nationals from Kentish Bus and Midland Red. The minibus fleet consisted of MCW Metroriders and Freight Rover Sherpas. Northumbria seemed to be quite a fan of Leyland Leopards for use on the long routes to Alnwick and Berwick. Five were rebodied in 1987 with

Duple 320 coachwork, which were stylish machines but notoriously cramped. Northumbria's coaching division also favoured Bova's and the mighty MCW Metroliner, a machine that had real presence but an indifferent reputation for reliability.

United's Pickering and Scarborough services went to East Yorkshire based at Analby Road, Hull. Named Scarborough & District, they operated in a neat but sober deep red and cream. The remaining United operations were centred on Cleveland, County Durham, and a large portion of North Yorkshire, including Hambleton, Richmondshire, Whitby and the Ripon portion of Harrogate District. Caldaire Holdings, the West Yorkshire-based owners of West Riding and Yorkshire Woollen, purchased United on 2 December 1987. The name Caldaire was a portmanteau of the words Aire and Calder – both West Yorkshire rivers.

United's fleet at the time had a rather faded and tired air. The Leyland Leopard coaches and Nationals looked especially shabby and time expired. The marketing of services was sometimes uninspiring and bus stations like the dingy Feethams, were not going to encourage motorists to desert their cars in favour of public transport. United were fortunate to inherit the lion's share of Mercedes-Benz L608D minibuses at deregulation. These were put to good use in Darlington and proved very durable. There was also a sizeable fleet of Renault-Dodge S56s and a largely forgotten batch of Fiat (Iveco) F49.10s. Apart from a batch of Plaxton-bodied Leyland Tiger coaches delivered in 1987, the first serious investment in new buses was in 1990 under Caldaire auspices. A batch of five Leyland Lynxes and five DAF SB220s were acquired for evaluation and were a massive improvement on the LHs, Leopards and Nationals. Incidentally some Mark 1 Nationals were re-engined with DAF units at this time including No. 1309, which was used as an evaluation vehicle.

In the meantime operations around Hartlepool, Teesside, Stokesley and Whitby were transferred to a new unit called Tees & District in February 1990. Services still reached as far as Helmsley, Newcastle and Scarborough. Tees & District buses were attired in a red, white and yellow livery. It looked vulgar, was difficult to keep clean and was sometimes inconsistently applied. Bristol VRs and Leyland Olympians looked especially unhappy in the original Tees livery. West Riding supplied several ageing VRs to boost the fleet strength. Considerable numbers of used Plaxton-bodied Leyland Tigers, from sources as varied as Eastern National, Luton & District and Trent, were used on inter-urban services. West Riding's relatively uncommon Alexander TE Tigers also joined the fleet, adding more interest to a cosmopolitan fleet.

The renamed and reconfigured TMS also came into Caldaire's orbit as Teesside Motor Services. TMS had been formerly known as Trimdon Motor Services and was a respected and successful independent. TMS traditionally kept a modern fleet, latterly Duple-bodied Leyland Leopards and Tigers. Before deregulation services reached Bishop Auckland, Bishopton, Coxhoe, Durham, Hartlepool, Horden, Stillington and Stockton-on-Tees. The company also had a successful holiday business called Zebra Holidays and a coach service to London named Blue Line. At deregulation the company expanded into the lucrative territory of Cleveland, Tyneside and Sunderland. The Bristol LH was the chassis of choice, being available, economical and reliable despite being designed with a short life expectancy. Bristol LHs had arrived from the likes of Crosville, Lincolnshire Road Car and Southern Vectis. Post-deregulation TMS had also tried the Leyland National, but found it thirsty, despite the easier access it offered elderly passengers. TMS were a thorn in the side of Busways, and especially Cleveland Transit. Many Transit drivers moved to TMS and those that didn't sometimes found themselves involved in bus-rage incidents on Stockton High Street. TMS also offered change where Transit was slow to abandon the unpopular 'exact fare' system.

The TMS operations were rationalised around 1989. Operations in Newcastle and Sunderland, known as TWOC (Tyne and Wear Omnibus Company), were acquired by Busways in November

1989. Most of the employees were made redundant as Busways saw no reason to continue with wasteful competition. Down in Teesside, TMS became Teesside Motor Services in April 1989. The operation became a part of Caldaire in April 1990, United operating many of the TMS Leopards and Tigers. In the 1990s, the fleet was dramatically transformed with the purchase of stylish Optare-bodied DAFs and MANs, although used Leyland Nationals would also make an appearance. Today all trace of TMS has been erased, apart from the depot at Boathouse Lane, Stockton-on-Tees, which is now used by Arriva.

In 1992, Caldaire sold off the United, Tees and TMS triumvirate under the title North East Bus. The ownership of United henceforth becomes somewhat convoluted. To cut to the chase, both United and Northumbria were acquired by the Cowie Group in 1996. Cowie had acquired Northumbria's owner British Bus and was best known as a motor dealer. Meanwhile, in 1992, Caldaire divested itself of United, who with Tees and TMS were now known as North East Bus. NEB endured a revolving door of owners – Westcourt, National Express and British Bus. In 1996, Bristish Bus passed to the expanding Cowie Group. With Northumbria and North East Bus now in the Cowie family, it effectively meant the reunification of United north of the Cleveland Hills. Officially Northumbria, Tees, TMS and United were separate entities, but it was an interesting turn of events. Cowie also sold the Ripon area services to Harrogate & District in 1996. In 1997, Cowie Group was renamed Arriva. The various North East operations were integrated, services rationalised and the age profile of the fleet further improved. Since 1994, the fleet had benefited from investment in Optare-bodied DAFs, MANs and Mercedes-Benz products, which had displaced the LHs, VRs and Nationals. Arriva North East is now officially Arriva Durham County with depots located at Alnwick (Lionheart Enterprise Park), Ashington, Belmont, Blyth, Dormanstown, Faverdale (Darlington), Jesmond, Stockton-on-Tees and Whitby.

Arriva's operations stretch from Berwick-upon-Tweed down to Scarborough, with the main focus being south-east Northumberland, most of County Durham and the Middlesbrough, Redcar and East Cleveland area, plus a share of the 685 into Cumbria. Services in Hexham are largely in the hands of Go North East, those in Berwick, Middleton-in-Teesdale and Wooler independents. There is little trace of continuity with United in North Yorkshire with the exception of services to Catterick Garrison, Richmond and Whitby. Many of the former United depots have closed since the 1990s – Alnwick, Berwick, Bishop Auckland, Durham (the scene of a terrible conflagration in 1979), Hartlepool, Loftus, Middlesbrough, Morpeth, Richmond, Ripon, Sunderland and so forth. Apart from the appearance of preserved buses, all trace of United has disappeared – even the odd surviving bus stop flag have been 'acquired' by zealous enthusiasts. A few depots survive, including the stately but shabby Jesmond garage at Portland Terrace, Newcastle. United House at Grange Road, Darlington, was dispensed with in 1994 and has been demolished. Eastern Counties is now known as First Norfolk & Suffolk with depots at Great Yarmouth, King's Lynn, Ipswich, Lowestoft and Norwich. Stagecoach operate the former Eastern Counties services in Cambridgeshire and Peterborough.

Based in Sunderland, Arriva has been owned by Deutsche Bahn since 2010. At the time of writing, press reports suggest Deutsche Bahn is intending to sell Arriva, which operates in fourteen countries across Europe.

Perth-based Stagecoach, one of the most successful bus operators to emerge from deregulation, has effectively sewn up the North East's former municipal companies – either by purchase (Cleveland Transit) or by hostile competition (Darlington). Stagecoach acquired Busways in July 1994, becoming the successor to Tyne and Wear PTE. Busways operations were centred on Newcastle, South Shields and Sunderland. Busways also took over the long-established Jolly service between South Hylton and Sunderland in June 1995.

Stagecoach acquired the much rationalised Cleveland Transit in September 1994. Cleveland Transit had been in existence since April 1974. Transit was the successor to Teesside Municipal Transport and before that Middlesbrough Corporation, Stockton Corporation and Teesside Railless Traction Board. Before being sold to her employees after deregulation, Transit had been owned by Langbaurgh, Middlesbrough and Stockton Councils. Hartlepool had remained proudly independent. The takeover of Transit brought with it Kingston upon Hull City Transport in what was then the intensely disliked Humberside. Transit's operations had been much reduced after deregulation with Guisborough, South Bank and Middlesbrough depots having been closed by 1991. Fleet and service reduction was severe and by late 1990 the VRs and a good proportion of the Fleetlines had departed. The rebodied Atlanteans from 1970 survived a little longer. Transit's fleet reduction was in no small part due to the intense competition from the likes of Delta, Robson of Thornaby, Tees & District, TMS and United. There had also been incursions from Escort and Nelson Line (Thornaby). Nevertheless, post-deregulation Transit had one of the most modern fleets in the country, a bright new livery and sound investments in new stock. In July 1995, Stagecoach Transit divested itself of Cleveland Coaches to Delta of Stockton. In return they acquired Delta's services. Stagecoach Teesside, the successor to Transit, now covers a compact area based on Billingham, Stockton-on-Tees and Middlesbrough. Services no longer penetrate Guisborough, Liverton Mines, Saltburn and other far-flung parts of the old Cleveland County.

Stagecoach purchased Hartlepool Transport in December 1994, and out went the attractive cream and maroon livery. It wasn't long before the much-loved Bristol REs were withdrawn from service or the somewhat unloved Dennis Falcons and Leyland Nationals. Until Stagecoach acquired Hartlepool, the fleet had been characterised by low levels of investment and a very inconsistent buying policy. Between 1977 and 1985 the undertaking never bought exactly the same bus twice. It seemed that nothing could replace the Bristol RE in Hartlepool's heart – certainly not the horrendously ungainly East Lancs-bodied Dennis Dominators. Hartlepool had shown little desire to expand its territory either, give or take an express service to Newcastle or occasional contract work to Middlesbrough and Stillington. Today, Stagecoach Hartlepool operate a small network of services around Hartlepool's estates serving places such as Clavering and The Fens. Service 1 crosses the Hartlepool boundary on the scenic route to Middlesbrough via Haverton Hill. It is worth noting that, until 1967, Hartlepool was two different entities with separate municipal bus companies. The year 1967 witnessed the merger of the distinct towns of Hartlepool and West Hartlepool plus their municipal fleets. Hartlepool Corporation did not begin bus operation until 1953, following a dispute with West Hartlepool Corporation. Stagecoach North East currently have depots at Hartlepool, Slatyford (Newcastle), South Shields, Stockton-on-Tees, Sunderland and Walkergate (Newcastle).

Darlington Transport disappeared from the bus scene in 1994 following a crippling bus war. After hanging on in the face of ferocious competition from United since 1986 – and later Your Bus – the Stagecoach incursion was just too much and the company folded on 9 November 1994. With perilous finances, Darlington Transport had been put up for sale in July 1994. There was interest from Badgerline, Stagecoach Busways and Yorkshire Traction, with the latter the leading bidder. Stagecoach Busways launched an assault on Darlington anyway, registering services and recruiting drivers, exacerbating an already tense bus war. I recall chaotic scenes as endless buses jostled for passengers. The air was acrid with diesel fumes and the streets positively hazardous for pedestrians. Stagecoach brought in a variety of buses including Leyland Nationals, Leyland Tigers and Fleetlines from Sunderland. At the start of November over half of Darlington's workforce had moved over to the new Stagecoach Darlington. Stagecoach buses being free at the point of use and bereft of manpower and revenue, Darlington Transport had no realistic chance of survival. The projected sale to Barnsley-based Yorkshire Traction having already collapsed, Stagecoach won the war by the back door. Stagecoach's free services served Darlington suburbs but also extended out to Catterick Garrison and Middlesbrough. Loadings were more than healthy and some bus enthusiasts thought they were in heaven. By 1995 PSV operations in Darlington had calmed, Your Bus selling out to West Midlands Travel on 16 December 1994, with Stagecoach and United then scaling back. Stagecoach sold the Darlington operation to Arriva in 2007 and ended up buying Yorkshire Traction in December 2005. The 'Tracky', as it was affectionately known, is as much missed in South Yorkshire as Darlington Transport in County Durham.

Arriva now has a virtual monopoly in Darlington and works out of a modern facility at Faverdale. The Darlington Corporation depot plus United's properties at Feethams and Grange Road have been demolished. Today, with most of Darlington town centre pedestrianised, and the rationalisation of bus services, it is easy to forget just how chaotic the town was between 1986 and early 1995.

Go North East is the region's home-grown titan. The Northern General Transport Company was founded in 1913 with the first depot located at Picktree Lane, Chester-le-Street. In 1914, the company absorbed Gateshead and District Tramways Co., Tynemouth and District Electric Traction Co., plus Jarrow and District Electric Traction Co. In 1931, Northern acquired Sunderland District Omnibus Co. In 1980 Northern painted several buses in heritage liveries. An example included Leyland National No. 4706, adorned in Sunderland District blue-and-white livery.

There were two bus stations opened in Newcastle at Marlborough Crescent and Worswick Street, plus expansion at Stanley and elsewhere. From about 1923, Northern constructed and designed its own bodywork, most notably the SE6. Between 1951 and 1953 Northern refurbished some elderly AEC Regals. This included the rather dramatic decision to extend the wheelbase. Experience in complex modifications later led to such extreme rebuilds as The Tynesider and Wearsider in 1972. Theoretically a Leyland Titan PD3 and AEC Routemaster, they were dramatically rebuilt and catastrophically ugly. More subtle modifications were carried out on Leyland Panthers and Nationals.

Northern were early users of the revolutionary Leyland Atlantean – the first rear engine double-decker chassis in Britain. Blame the Leyland Atlantean if you miss bus conductors! Northern's final new Atlanteans arrived in 1980 and carried handsome Roe bodywork. A dramatic purchase in 1982 was fifty MCW examples from Tyne and Wear PTE. These were the last bodies constructed by MCW before they concentrated production on their own designs – the Metrobus, Metroliner and Metrorider.

Northern, along with United, joined the newly formed National Bus Company on 1 January 1969. Venture Transport of Consett was acquired in 1970 with eighty-six buses. The individual identities of existing subsidiaries such as Sunderland District and Tyneside were gradually phased out in the 1970s. Standard NBC colours did not become mandatory until 1972. In the heyday of NBC control, Northern had two main liveries. Buses operating within the Tyne and Wear Metropolitan County were painted NBC yellow and, from 1981, PTE yellow. Vehicles within County Durham were resplendent in NBC poppy red. Northern's diverse fleet (683 in 1984) operated in a compact but populous urban area bounded roughly by Blyth, Consett, Durham, Newcastle and Seaham. Services did, of course, reach Crook, Darlington, Esh Winning, Hartlepool, Middlesbrough and elsewhere. United, who had 811 buses in 1984, had, as previously mentioned, operations stretching between the Scottish Borders region and West Yorkshire. In preparation for deregulation in 1986, the name Go-Ahead Northern was adopted. Some buses appeared in a rainbow livery with the slogan 'Don't judge a bus by its colour – read the name!' Many casual bus passengers were probably none the wiser about Northern having a red and a yellow fleet. Additionally, the abolition of Tyne and Wear County in 1986 resulted in a significant loss of subsidies to Northern.

Northern's NBC era fleet was always interesting. The Bristol VRs had the less common Leyland engines in lieu of the Gardner 6XLB. Most had high-bridge ECW, or rare Willowbrook bodywork. The Atlanteans carried ECW, Park Royal and Roe bodies. There was also the 33-foot Atlanteans from Tyne and Wear PTE, which had Alexander or MCW bodywork. Fifteen MCW Metrobuses arrived in 1980, followed by more in 1984 and 1986. There was also the usual mixture of Leopards, Nationals and Olympians. On the coaching front Leyland Royal Tigers Nos 7012–7013 and the badly designed ECW-bodied Leopards (Nos 7097–7100) added further interest for enthusiasts.

Northern was privatised in February 1987 following a partial management buyout, led by the late Martin Ballinger. After a cautious approach to deregulation and some industrial unrest, Northern quickly became adept at marketing their services with savvy advertising – such as 'This is Go-Ahead Northern Country'. The title Go-Ahead Group was adopted as the company moniker and PTE yellow disappeared from the roads of Tyne and Wear. Red and white became the standard livery but all that was to change in 1992 when various brand names were introduced. Everything from the colourful Value for Money buses in South Tyneside, the more sombre Coastline in North Tyneside, the dynamic Wear Buses in Sunderland district and the more traditional red of Northern around north Durham. Go-Ahead went from strength to strength, investing in new stock, purchasing other firms such as Gypsy Queen (1989), Low Fell Coaches (1992), Armstrongs of Ebchester (1995), Diamond (1995), OK Travel (1995) and further afield Brighton & Hove (1993), Oxford Bus Company (1994), etc. They have a presence in London, too, with London Central (1994), London General (1996) and Metrobus (1999).

The post-deregulation period witnessed more rationalisation in the North East with the closure of High Spen, Jarrow, Murton, Park Lane, Philadelphia, Stanley and Winlaton depots. Even Sunderland Road depot at Gateshead has bitten the dust. Later respected brands like OK Travel were put out to pasture while others such as Diamond and Venture have been revived. Keeping their image fresh, Go-Ahead Group North East, became Go North East and changed their livery again in 1998. The blue, red and yellow looked effective, presenting a dynamic and fresh image for the Gateshead firm.

Today's Go North East is an eclectic range of buses and complex branding schemes. Committed bus enthusiasts won't have any problems differentiating, but those with a relatively perfunctory interest like myself are likely to be bamboozled. That said, the services are reliable, the buses always well-presented and the branding imaginative – Angel, Red Kite, Tyne Valley Ten and X-Lines, etc. Go North East have even resurrected the pre-deregulation rainbow livery to promote diversity. At the time of writing Go North East's operating territory is notable for its expansion. Services now reach Linton and Cambois, traditionally United and Northumbria territory. Likewise Allendale Town, Birdoswald (Cumbria), Haltwhistle, Hexham, Prudhoe and Wark, once the preserve of independents or United, now see Go North East buses. Arriva sold their Hexham operations to Go North East in 2010. I still can't quite accept seeing a Go North East bus around Haydon Bridge or Wall; they still look alien to me. At the time of writing Go North East have depots at Chester-le-Street, Deptford (Sunderland), Hexham, Hownsgill (Consett), Percy Main, Peterlee, Riverside, Saltmeadows and Washington. The company continues to go from strength to strength with a listing on the London Stock Exchange and transport investments in Germany, Norway, the Republic of Ireland and Singapore. There are also numerous operations within the UK including Go East Anglia, Go North West

(Cheetham Hill, Manchester), Go South Coast, Plymouth Citybus, and Southeastern trains. Quite an achievement for a North East-based company.

One unfortunate change that was already apparent in the 1990s is the decline and disappearance of independent bus companies. The buses, liveries and services of operators such as Bond Bros (Willington), The Eden (sold to United in 1995 but since resurrected by Grahams Motor Services, West Auckland), Rochester & Marshall, Trimdon Motor Services and, of course, OK Travel are much missed. There really isn't that much variety on the independent scene today, but let's be grateful for what we have. Scarlet Band of West Cornforth play an important role within County Durham. The same can be said of JH Coaches at Birtley, Borders Buses at Berwick-upon-Tweed, Glendale at Wooler and Travelsure at Belford, etc. The erstwhile Optare Solo is a favourite of both the independents and the majors. Old buses these days tend to be in better shape after fifteen years of hard graft, as can be evidenced by a cursory glance at Weardale's smart fleet. The era of high-stepped, rackety and environmentally unfriendly buses is fast becoming a thing of the past. Nevertheless, the LHs, REs, VRs, Atlanteans and Nationals, etc., had great character.

Character is one thing modern buses seem to lack. Modern engines lack melody and the body designs tend to be bland (Temsa Avenue) or plain ugly (Plaxton Primo). Construction methods also make many buses appear fragile. The Mercedes Citaro, a successful design I actually admire, looks somewhat flimsy, like some overgrown toy bus that could easily break apart. However, appearance and reality are not the same thing – Leyland Nationals looked robust but were often unreliable and dicey in the wet. Modern buses also lack the melodic sounds of yore. No more do cities ring to the roar and clatter of a Leyland 510 or 680 engine. But progress is progress, and buses are designed to give passengers a good experience and operators a healthy profit margin, not serve the whims of a bus enthusiast. The introduction of hybrid and gas buses adds an extra dimension of interest too, as well as pleasing the green lobby.

Adventurous colour schemes and route branding is very much the norm today. I personally prefer 'traditional' two-tone liveries, such as Darlington's blue and cream, but they are persona non grata in the current marketing climate. Some complex liveries work, such as Go North East's Cobalt & Coast, others look less convincing such as the Black Cats. Incidentally, I did like Northumbria's grey, red and white, even when it looked overdone on some of their Leopards. In whatever style, I've never been a great admirer of Stagecoach liveries, although the new schemes are better than the previous examples. As for Arriva, I am somewhat undecided. I think it depends on whether the sun is shining. I have also lost count of how many route-branded buses operate totally away from their designated routes, something which is perhaps inevitable.

Many bus stations have been redeveloped or closed since the 1990s. Gallowgate, Marlborough Crescent, Park Lane (Sunderland), Central Bus Station (Sunderland) and Whitley Bay have been raised. Worswick Street, Newcastle, once notorious for congestion, is facing demolition, having been closed for years. Blaydon, Consett and Haymarket have been modernised. Brand new structures – some of them absolutely awful – have replaced earlier designs, too. Park Lane Interchange is messy, Peterlee acceptable and workmanlike, Hexham ugly but useful and Ashington is just bus stands and tarmac – really nothing at all.

The growth of car ownership in the North East, traditionally a region that lagged behind regions such as the South East or West Midlands, has impacted on bus usage. Likewise limited subsidies, rationalisation and operators' unwillingness to service loss-making routes means there are fewer buses around these days. This is most noticeable in the bus stations themselves. Middlesbrough bus station seems positively low key these days, Park Lane Interchange oversized and Hexham just about right. Stockton-on-Tees, which can claim to have the longest and widest High Street in the UK, looks rather bare these days. Gone are the sea of buses, market stalls and shoppers of the past. Bishop Auckland, once the Mecca for independent operators, is but a shadow of its former self, the disappearance of the bus operators paralleling the decline of the local economy.

North East Buses Today is a snapshot of the current PSV scene in the region. It is not exhaustive, nor is it meant to be a fleet-list guide or comprehensive analysis of bus operators. I have tried to include a variety of places around the region so no subdivision is excluded. Apologies to places such as Amble, Middleton-in-Teesdale, Peterlee, Redcar, Tynemouth and Wallsend for missing you out.

The big event hovering over the production of this book was the Covid-19 pandemic. Observance of social distancing brought any chance of photographs to a halt at the end of March 2020. The last few pictures before lockdown were taken around Cockfield and Tow Law. I cannot recall such a strange and unsettling atmosphere in my lifetime. I was able to resume my photography as the lockdown was eased in July. I discarded one picture at Coulby Newham showing a line of people with face coverings – they looked like something out of a George A. Romero movie, *c.* 1978. It was a surreal sight, who would have thought bussing would be so different in 2020? Another unused shot shows a deserted Chester-le-Street – it was like being on the set of *The Omega Man*. I was expecting Charlton Heston to get off the bus shouting 'And you survived, too?' Those with a desire to see buses operating in lockdown should subscribe to Dave Spencer on YouTube. The PMP founder has intriguing footage of Gateshead, Newcastle, South Shields, Canterbury, Chatham, Hemel Hempstead and elsewhere.

I hope you enjoy this collection of photographs of *North East Buses Today*. My photographs are not works of art but I hope they give a nice flavour of the current bus scene. They should be interesting to look back on in 2120.

I would like to thank John Bailey for proofreading the text and all at Amberley Publishing. Finally, any errors in this book are mine. All photographs are by the author unless otherwise stated.

A colourful line up of Go North East Buses at Stanley bus station in the summer of 2016. Liveries on display include Lime, Diamond and traditional Northern red.

No. 99 is a Dennis Loline/ Northern Counties combination new in 1958. Preserved in her original Middlesbrough Corporation livery, she is seen on wedding duties at Middlegate, Hartlepool, in 2016. The Loline was a licence-built version of the Bristol Lodekka, supplied to municipal operators and companies outside the state-owned sector.

Barnard Castle is one of County Durham's most visually arresting towns. Situated on the river Tees, the town is home to the remarkable French-style Bowes Museum. In recent years, 'Barney' has become famous as a place for spin doctors to test their eyesight. Captured on layover in May 2018 was this Optare Solo, YJ55 YGH, operated by Scarlet Band of West Cornforth.

Stanhope is considered the capital of Weardale, one of northern England's lesser-known, but most enthralling, valleys. Weardale's VDL SB180/MCV Evolution was photographed at Stanhope, working the long-established Bishop Auckland service in August 2016.

Shadforth is a somewhat prepossessing village within Durham's former colliery country. Of historical interest are the Iron Age and Bronze Age sites in the area. There are also quarries at Crime Rigg and Witch Hill. On a humid August day in 2018, an unidentified Arriva Wright Streetlite passes through Shadforth's main street en route to Hartlepool.

Arriva No. 1914 is a DAF SB120/Wright Cadet new in 2000. The bus exudes a tired air as it enters High Street, Stockton-on-Tees, in August 2018. No. 1914 was withdrawn from Stockton depot in 2019.

At the other end of the North East is Lindisfarne, often referred to as Holy Island, and in rare cases as Islandshire. Woody's Taxis and Executive Travel of Berwick-upon-Tweed were operating a shuttle service between Lindisfarne Castle and the village centre on 6 September 2019. YX59 DZB is a Volkswagen Transporter/Blubird Tucana combination first registered in February 2010.

Sedgefield was made world famous as the parliamentary seat of Prime Minister Tony Blair. The constituency also contains the larger settlement of Newton Aycliffe, plus villages such as Archdeacon Newton, Fishburn and Hurwoth. Arriva No. 4807, a MAN 19.270EcoCity/ Caetano was photographed at Durham Road on 4 November 2019. The bus would normally be used on the Frequenta service in Darlington, which connects Branksome with Red Hall.

Pictured at Thornley Station is Garnett's Coaches X288 NNO. New to Stagecoach East London, she is a Dennis Trident/Alexander combination new in 2001. Garnetts are based at Tindale Crescent near Bishop Auckland and operate several school contracts in County Durham using yellow buses.

Lanchester is an affluent village between Consett and Durham. All Saints Church and Longovicium Roman fort, constructed around AD 122, make Lanchester an interesting place to perambulate. Passing through Front Street on 3 February 2020 is Go North East's No. 6159. New to London General, she is a Volvo B9TL/Wright Gemini.

At the time of writing, service 81 between Redcar and Stokesley, had been bifurcated. Arriva No. 4516 had just set down a passenger at Fishponds Road, Yearby, when the service was still complete, on 8 February 2020.

Southwick has been subsumed by the northward expansion of Sunderland. There are still faint echoes of a village atmosphere around the Green, despite the city centre being a short distance away. Representing insensitive post-war redevelopment around Beaumont Street and Sunderland Road, two Stagecoach single-deckers are caught at work in early 2020. Nearest the camera is No. 39710, a MAN 14.240 LF with Alexander Enviro200 bodywork.

Go North East are very progressive when it comes to marketing their services. This, in turn, provides much interest for enthusiasts and confusion for those who can't stay abreast with the changes. At Framwellgate Moor, Xlines No. 6331 works the X21 into Durham. The bus is a Wright StreetDeck, new in 2017.

Photographed at Raby Road in what had been West Hartlepool until 1967 is Arriva No. 1412, VDL SB200/Wright Pulsar 2 combination new in March 2009. The towns of Hartlepool and West Hartlepool were merged in 1967. Hartlepool gained extra territory including Dalton Piercy, Hart and Newton Bewley as a result of local government reorganisation in April 1974.

No. 26291 is an Alexander Dennis Enviro 200 MMC, new in 2019. The convoluted designations given to modern buses contrast sharply with the simpler names of the past – AEC Swift, Bristol LH and Leyland Panther, et al. No. 26291 was photographed between Hardwick and Roseworth at Durham Road, Stockton-on-Tees.

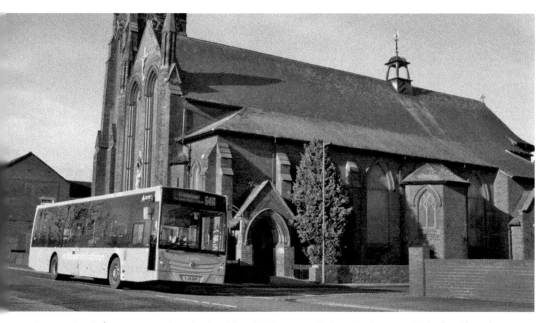

On a crisp February morning Arriva No. 4707 passes St Peter's Roman Catholic Church at South Bank. The settlement has seen considerable industrial decline, depopulation and the demolition of poor-quality housing stock in the past few decades. The bus is an odd sounding Temsa Avenue, working the 64A to Grangetown.

An atmospheric shot of Stagecoach No. 27242 at Norton following heavy rain. Norton is famed locally for its attractive houses and beautiful green despite being in close proximity to heavy industry. The original 'Big Ben' bell was cast at Norton Foundry in 1856. After testing in London, the bell cracked and George Mears of Whitechapel was contracted to forge the new tocsin.

Representing Stagecoach's new 'Ocean green' livery for specialist services is No. 11157, an Alexander Dennis Enviro 400MC, branded Cross Pennine for service 685 between Carlisle and Newcastle. Photographed at Blucher Village, she is based at Carlisle and is part of the Stagecoach Cumbria & North Lancashire division.

County Durham is often referred to as 'the land of the Prince Bishops'. The bishops of Durham once exercised considerable power on behalf of the medieval monarchs, the area being known as the Palatine of Durham. Appropriately enough, Go North East No. 5424 carries Prince Bishops branding for service 20 at West Rainton.

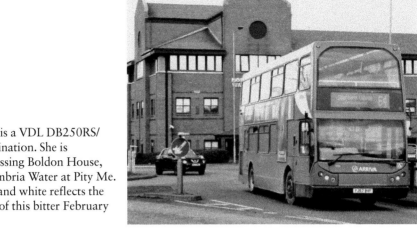

Arriva No. 7455 is a VDL DB250RS/ East Lancs combination. She is photographed passing Boldon House, home of Northumbria Water at Pity Me. The harsh black and white reflects the grime and damp of this bitter February day in 2020.

A black and white shot of a desolate Shotton Colliery in March 2020. Arriva No. 1533 is working service 22 to Durham. Nearby is the new town of Peterlee (1948), designed to alleviate unemployment and provide a better environment for people moving away from East Durham's colliery villages.

The steep incline at Hall Road, West Chopwell, presents no problems for Go North East's Red Kite branded No. 6119. This sturdy Volvo B9TL/ Wright Eclipse Gemini 2 is working the X47 to Newcastle. Despite being in Gateshead district, Chopwell, perhaps surprisingly, has a Newcastle postcode.

Speeding out of Skinningrove, No. 1444 is one of numerous VDL SB200/Wright Pulsar 2s in the Arriva fleet. Services in East Cleveland are always operated by single-deckers due to the large number of low bridges.

Climbing the steep Loftus Bank into Carlin How is No. 1572, a Wright SteetLite Micro-Hybrid. In the background, Skinningrove Beck winds through the foot of the valley with the town of Loftus at the top. The railway bridge carries the mineral line to Boulby. Many of the roads in this part of East Cleveland are steeply graded, and Loftus Bank has been very susceptible to erosion in recent years.

Coatham Coaches of Margrove Park were operating this fine Mercedes-Benz Tourismo on 10 February 2020. In heavy rain BN11 UGF peregrinates Dunsdale probably to collect scholars in the Redcar area.

Service 35 between Stockton and Billingham (Wolviston Court) is normally operated by single-deckers. Stagecoach No. 19205 passes Norton's expansive and aesthetically pleasing green in February 2020. The bus is an ADL Enviro400, new in 2007.

The Wright Solar body fitted to this Scania L94UB is an elegant and timeless design. Go North East No. 5208 dates from 2004 and appeared to be in pristine condition when photographed at Hetton-le-Hole in March 2020. Sadly, Wright Solar operation ended on 17 July 2020.

Traversing the B1280 at Station Town in blazing sunlight is Arriva No. 4811. The villages around Station Town are predominantly former colliery settlements such as Thornley, Wheatley Hill and Wingate. The area is rich in former railway lines too including the Hart to Haswell Walkway.

One of Go North East's fine Volvo B9TLs was captured heading towards Houghton-le-Spring at Philadelphia on 2 February 2020. Out of view is the site of the former Northern depot at Philadelphia, which closed in 1989. Services from 'Philly' once reached as far as Hartlepool and Ryton.

Representing Stagecoach's commitment to environmental issues is No. 28018. The bus in question is a cumbersomely named Scania K270UB/Alexander Dennis Enviro 300NG. She was photographed amid rush hour traffic at Town End Farm in Sunderland.

Technically Wright Bros of Nenthead should be in a north-west edition of this book. However, the fleet can often be seen in Northumberland and Pennine areas of County Durham. KIW 989, a Volvo B12M with Jonckheere bodywork, was photographed at Holeyn Hall near Horsley on a teatime run.

Arriva No. 7537, a Dennis Trident 2/Alexander Enviro400, has just entered Durham Road for the climb up to Ferryhill town centre. Situated on a limestone escarpment, the Ferryhill area is famous for mining and quarrying. The best-known mine, the Dean & Chapter Colliery, closed in 1966.

Clara Vale is a small and rather secluded village on the south bank of the River Tyne. Bus services have been reduced in recent years, although Gateshead Central Taxis were using this Fiat Ducato/Bluebird Orion Plus combination. Service R3 is operated on behalf of Nexus, the name for Transport for Tyne and Wear.

No. 6162 is a Scania N94UD/East Lancs OmniDekka working for Go North East. Photographed at Langley Park, she was new to Brighton & Hove. In 1989, Northern acquired the small operator Gypsy Queen, who operated a fleet of Bedfords from their Langley Park base.

Weardale's red and white livery looks very smart on this Transbus Trident/ Transbus ALX400. Carrying the registration plate SN03 EBK, she was on school bus duties at Hunwick in February 2020.

High Spen was once home to a Venture Transport depot. The Consett-based operator, the largest independent in the region, sold out to Northern General in 1970. Go North East's Tyne Valley Ten branded Volvo B9TL/Wright Eclipse Gemini 2 leaves Glossop Street, High Spen, for Newcastle.

Here is another one of those ubiquitous Optare Solos. Perhaps to be avoided, No. 666 represents Go North East's Indigo branding in South Hetton. Close to this site stood the grim Hawthorn Coking Plant (Murton Coking Plant).

Breaking the monotony of Stagecoach's corporate colours is this fine Scania K270UB/Enviro 300NG. With an impending shower forecast, No. 28021 brightens up the environs of Southwick in 2020.

Working the Gateshead Loop at Shields Road, Felling, is Go North East No. 6122. The Gateshead district has a fascinating variety of architectural styles, especially in the sphere of social housing. Some of the more extreme examples such as Clasper Village, St Cuthbert's Estate and Derwent Tower ('The Dunston Rocket') have now been demolished.

The driver of Stagecoach No. 12079, a Dennis Trident 2/Alexander Enviro400, checks his cell phone while on layover at Newburn Road, Throckley. The bus will pass virtually the full length of Newcastle before arrival at the Cobalt Business Park in North Tyneside.

Willington was once home to Bond Bros, who operated a small fleet of pale blue and cream buses to Wear Valley View, Sunnybrow and Oakenshaw. The fleet in 1986 included six AEC Reliances, four Bedfords and a Bristol LH. In March 2020, the Wear Valley View service was being operated by Scarlet Band using this former Transdev, Optare Versa. The location is Willington, County Durham.

East Hedleyhope is an attractively sited former mining village near Esh Winning. Highlighting the problems of rural transport, service 52 serves an isolated community, is infrequent and, in this shot, was leaving the village bereft of passengers. The Solo is operated by Scarlet Band, but came from Go North East via Plymouth Citybus.

The same bus as it enters the neighbouring settlement of Waterhouses. Note the charming terraced bungalows known as Ivesley Cottages, quite typical of parts of County Durham. Two passengers boarded at Waterhouses for Durham.

Despite the reduction in bus services over the years transport enthusiasts can still find plenty of activity at Heworth Metro. Two Mercedes-Benz Citaros in The Crusader branding, a Solo and Verso, can be seen on this gloomy March day. Out of shot are the railway lines carrying the Metro and diesel trains on 7 March 2020.

Close to the Northumberland boundary and a few miles west of Consett is the village of Castleside. Go North East No. 5450 collects a sole passenger at Church Street, Castleside, for the teatime run to Durham.

Transporting morning commuters to Sunderland is this neat little Wright StreetLite DF, No. 5375 in the Go North East fleet. The location is Ryhope, which is situated close to the North Sea and alongside the preserved Ryhope Pumping Station (1866–70).

Making a tight turn off the A167 (Great North Road) into Ferryhill is this stylish Optare Versa. New to Lancashire United, she is working Scarlet Band's 8:45 a.m. service 113 from Bishop Auckland to Sedgefield.

Bates Avenue, Darlington. presents a degree of danger to bus drivers and pedestrians. The road is bendy, narrow and populated with parked cars. Arriva Optare Solo No. 2689 negotiates Friday evening rush-hour traffic and driving rain during March 2020.

A trio of Stagecoach buses are seen at Chichester Metro station in March 2020. Nearest to the camera is No. 27726, followed by No. 37307 and the rear of No. 39703. South Shields has one of England's longest established ethnic populations – the Yemeni community.

Advertising the merits of a £12 family day ticket, Go North East's No. 5420 was captured at rest in Houghton-le-Spring, Tyne and Wear. At its heart an interesting town with some significant old buildings, Houghton-le-Spring was effectively split in two by the construction of the A690 dual carriageway. The road links Sunderland with Crook via a steep cutting at Houghton-le-Spring.

Many companies are keen to support equality issues by painting vehicles in rainbow colours and slogans extolling the virtues of diversity. Looking relatively restrained compared to some designs, Go North East's No. 5292 is photographed at Grangetown on the southern edge of Sunderland.

German firm Mercedes-Benz spent years trying to break into the British PSV market having had considerable success with cars and commercial vehicles since the 1960s. In the 1990s they started to gain market share in the PSV sector, helped by large orders from Travel West Midlands. Go North East No. 5314 was photographed at Hebburn in South Tyneside.

Blackhall Mill is a pretty location by the River Derwent. The river forms the boundary between the old Tyne and Wear Metropolitan County and the revised Durham County. At the narrow riverside terminus is Go North East No. 6160. A Volvo B9TL/Wright combination, she was previously with Go-Ahead London.

Above Blackhall Mill is the former colliery village of Chopwell. The community was given the sobriquet 'Little Moscow' due to local support for the Communist Party in the 1920s. At the bus stance is Toon Link branded No. 6150. A short jaunt away, one can find Lenin Terrace and Marx Terrace, plus the distinctly Conservative-sounding Disraeli Terrace.

Blaydon Racer Mercedes-Benz Citaro No. 5276 arrives at Sunniside in March 2020. Nearby are the Tanfield Railway and the historic Causey Arch of 1725–26, the oldest surviving single-arch railway bridge in the world.

A nice shot of Stagecoach No. 22424 leaving Slatyford depot in Newcastle. The bus is one of the diminishing numbers of MAN/Alexander combinations in service. The bus was previously with Stagecoach Sheffield.

What a gas at Sunderland! Stagecoach No. 28019, one of several 'Gas Buses' operating in Wearside, departs Allendale Road, Farringdon, with a reasonable load in March 2020.

Dumpling Hall is an intriguing name for a housing estate. Located in Lemington, the residential estate is named after the eponymous hall which has since been demolished. Stagecoach No. 11288 was photographed at the terminus before departure to Walker via Byker.

On a fine March evening, Go North East No. 5361 passes along Sheddon's Hill near Eighton Banks. The Mercedes-Benz Citaro was working back to the depot at Washington. The historic Bowes Railway, *Angel of the North* and Tyne Marshalling Yard are located close to this hilly area.

One of the hazards of photographing buses today is being unable to capture their electronic destination boards. A case in point is No. 6162 as it works service 34A towards Perkinsville. The location is, of course, Ouston, County Durham.

Crossing the river Skerne at Parkside, Darlington, is this splendid Scania CN94UB/Scania Omnicity working service X26. Quakers, railways and engineering firms such as Cleveland Bridge brought great prosperity to this handsome town. Close to Parkside is Grange Road, where United Automobile Services were headquartered from 1932.

Seaham Harbour, now usually referred to as plain Seaham, was developed as a port by Charles Vane, 3rd Marquess of Londonderry in 1828. After years of decline following the closure of the pits at Dawdon, Seaham Colliery and Vane Tempest, the town is undergoing a mild renaissance. Go North East Optare Solo No. 637 collects passengers near the harbour in March 2020.

Go North East's Mercedes-Benz Citaro No. 5337 collects patrons at Blackhall Colliery in March 2020. The old Hardwick Hotel looks like it has seen better days but is still an interesting period piece. Nearby is the stunning East Durham coastline, which has been cleaned up after years of pollution from the mining industry.

A lonesome Stagecoach driver trainer bus, No. 22075, was pictured at Stockton-on-Tees depot in March 2020. The Portrack Lane depot was opened in 1965 by Stockton Corporation before passing to Teesside Municipal Transport, Cleveland Transit and finally Stagecoach.

Passing through Whiteleas on the edge of South Shields is Go North East's Scania Omnicity No. 5254. She was new in 2007 and was based at Washington when photographed in March 2020. Scania have built up considerable PSV sales in the UK since the 1970s. Leicester, London Transport, Merseyside PTE, Newport, Reading and, of course, Tyne and Wear PTE were early users of the brand.

The villages around Bishop Auckland once abounded with independent bus operators such as OK Motor Services, Bond Bros of Willington and Lockey of St Helen Auckland – all sadly defunct. Representing the modern corporate order is Arriva No. 1525 working service 6 to Bishop Auckland. The location is Evenwood, which had been Teesdale District until local government reorganisation in 2009.

Photographed at Cockfield is this neat little ADL Enviro in service with Scarlet Band. The bus was new to Britannia Parking of Bournemouth before being used on Durham Park & Ride services. Cockfield was the birthplace of the surveyor and astronomer Jeremiah Dixon. With Charles Mason, Dixon helped solve a famous boundary dispute in Colonial America with the Mason-Dixon Line (1763–67).

Bedlington Station, although officially in Northumberland, is historically a detached part of County Durham called Bedlingtonshire. Other detached parts of Durham were Craikshire, Islandshire and Norhamshire. Arriva's stylish No. 7547 has just alighted passengers at Ravensworth Street, Bedlington Station.

Stanhope Street, Arthurs Hill, is a vibrant, multiracial district of Newcastle comprising long rows of terraced streets and post-war social housing. The area has numerous churches, mosques and temples. Passengers disembark Stagecoach No. 12068, with electric hybrid lettering during 2020.

Toft Hill used to be served by OK Motor Services (OK Travel) with buses as diverse as the 1980 Dennis Dominator TUP104V and the 1962 Bedford VAS1. More mundane transport today is Arriva No. 1477 passing along the A68 at Toft Hill. The journey will include the former Category D village of Witton Park and Escomb, famous for an early Saxon church.

A quartet of Go North East buses are seen on layover at Consett bus station. Nearest the camera and the sole double-decker is No. 6917. Go North East opened a new £3.5 million depot at Hownsgill in 2019, which was constructed on part of the former Consett Steel Works.

There was just one female passenger waiting to board service 733 as it approached the remote settlement of Townfield, County Durham, in March 2020. Situated just outside Hunstanworth, Townfield is situated on the wild moors of north-west Durham close to the Northumberland boundary.

Appearing in exemplary condition for a 56 registration bus, Stagecoach No. 35188 is one of a disappearing breed of Dennis Darts SLFs. First registered in October 2006, she is seen entering Brockley Whins, South Tyneside, in March 2020.

Tees Flex is an on-demand service operated by Stagecoach. Serving villages such as Brafferton, Low Dinsdale and Wolviston, these distinctive blue buses can be seen around the Tees Valley. Prospective passengers need an app and credit or debit card. Photographed at the OK Diner on the A19, near Elwick, are two of the Mercedes-Benz Sprinters used on this innovative service.

Working off its normal haunt due to the onset of Covid-19 was Go North East's No. 5403, a Coast & Country branded Wright Streetlite. The location is Kibblesworth, Tyne and Wear. Nearby is the village of Lamesley, famous as the location of the once mighty Tyne Marshalling Yard.

Alnwick is a fine stone-built town that attracts thousands of tourists in the summer. Attractions include Alnwick Castle, Alnwick Garden and Barter Books. Passing the old railway station is this neat Optare Solo in service with Glen Valley Tours of Wooler. The Solo was new to Country Lion of Northampton in 2010.

Belford is a former coaching town, just off the A1, in the former Berwick-upon-Tweed district of Northumberland. Travelsure have a depot in the town that is also served by Arriva, the successor of both Northumbria and United Automobile Services. Travelsure were using this cheerful-looking Optare Solo on service 418 between Belford and Alnwick in March 2020.

One of the more interesting names for a bus operator in the North East is NEED Ltd. North East Equality and Diversity, based in Alnwick, is a charity providing community transport. Many vehicles are wheelchair accessible, including this Peugeot Boxer at Belford in March 2020.

Crossing from Tweedmouth into Berwick-upon-Tweed is Borders Buses No. 11323. She is working service 267 over the Royal Tweed Bridge, into what some proud Scots would still call Berwickshire.

Berwick-upon-Tweed is a fascinating town architecturally, historically and socially. This photograph was little more than a grab shot as Borders Buses Optare Solo passed under Scots Gate in March 2020. The bus was working the town service between Highcliffe and Spittal.

Cyclists and tourists were out in force at Felton, Northumberland, in March 2020. Arriva No. 7516 provides both comfort and excellent views for the tiny number of passengers patronising the X15 to Morpeth and Newcastle. The River Coquet separates Felton from the neighbouring community of West Thirston.

A communications mast intrudes on this photograph of two Stagecoach double-deckers at rest in Rhodes Street, Walker. No. 19219 is nearest the camera as the driver has a well-deserved puff in Newcastle-upon-Tyne, March 2020.

A number of spoiled but still salvageable classical terraces can be seen as Stagecoach No. 26278 approaches High Street, Stockton-on-Tees. The town's former industries included iron and steel production, shipbuilding and the construction of locomotives including the unreliable Class 28 diesel 'Metrovicks' built at Bowesfield Works.

Coxhoe is typical of County Durham's former colliery villages with long rows of terrace houses and gaps where buildings have been pulled down. The famed poet Elizabeth Barrett Browning spent her childhood at the now demolished Coxhoe Hall. Photographed outside St Joseph's Roman Catholic Church is this Arriva Solo No. 2822.

Bowburn is another former mining village a few miles south of Durham. New house building and cheap student accommodation keeps the village buoyant. Arriva No. 1415 passes the severe-looking terraces on Durham Road, Bowburn.

The design of the Wright Streetlite WF elicits a mixture of responses. Although aesthetically challenged, they are nevertheless practical for PSV work. Operated by JH Coaches of Birtley, MX61 BBU was caught at Dairy Lane, Houghton-le-Spring, during March 2020. The bus was new to Britannia Parking and also spent time with Roxburghshire-based Peter Hogg of Jedburgh.

Washington has numerous industrial estates, including Armstrong and Wear. Go North East have a depot at the rather unimaginatively named Industrial Road, Hertburn. Parked in the entrance is Mercedes-Benz Citaro No. 5485, just before it was placed on SORN (Statutory off Road Notification) as a result of service reductions due to Covid-19.

Go North East No. 6086 is painted in a special poppy-themed livery to commemorate military personnel who have died in conflicts. Tastefully attired in white with red poppies in support of the Royal British Legion during 2018, No. 6086 is seen departing Concord.

Killingworth Township, now known as plain Killingworth or 'Killy' by locals, was developed as a new town in 1963. An unidentified Arriva bus leaves the bus station and enters Citidal East. Despite branding for service 306, she was actually working a North Tyneside local.

Go North East No. 719 makes its way gingerly through Quaking Houses. Service 30 links Lanchester and Stanley in what was previously the Derwentside district of County Durham.

Working service 23 at Thorndale Road, Thorney Close, is Stagecoach No. 35189. Sunderland has numerous large housing schemes including Ford Estate and Plains Farm, which require regular bus services to accommodate high levels of patronage.

Leaving Mill Lane, Billingham, on service 34 to Owington Farm is Stagecoach No. 27510, a Dennis Enviro300/Alexander combination. The estate in the background is situated next to the much-depleted former ICI works.

Go North East's Red Arrows livery is seen to good effect as No. 6054 reaches the end of its journey from Newcastle. The location is Easington Lane (Clock), a village that straddles the border between County Durham and Sunderland.

The sylvan setting is Nuns Moor, part of a vast expanse of green space to the north of Newcastle city centre, often generically referred to as the Town Moor. The bus is a 2011 Dennis Dart SLF4/Alexander Enviro200 approaching Fenham on service 36.

Working into Teesside on the Sunday X10 service is Go North East No. 6310. New in 2017, she carries Wright Eclipse Gemini 3 bodywork mounted to a Volvo B5TL chassis. The location is Wolviston Road, Billingham.

A rear view of Arriva No. 1418 (VDL SB200/Wright Pulsar 2) as it enters the Arriva depot at Stockton-on-Tees. Close to Boathouse Lane is the River Tees and the historically significant St John's Crossing associated with the Stockton & Darlington Railway of 1825.

Station Road, Easington Colliery, is the location for Arriva No. 7562. Much of the 2000 film *Billy Elliot* was shot in Easington Colliery. The village pit lost eighty-three men following a mining explosion on 29 May 1951. The mine closed in 1993.

Go North East No. 5438, a Wright Streetlite DF, is photographed at Low Moorsley on a beautiful April evening. The bus is about to make the return journey back to Heworth Metro, Felling.

The Covid-19 lockdown resulted in bus and train services being reduced in frequency and in some cases stopped altogether. Go North East replaced their usual Wright double-deckers with this more efficient Dennis Dart SLF 5/Alexander Enviro 200MMC combination. No. 5490, sporting Green Arrow livery for route 97 in Gateshead, was photographed at Station Road, Billingham, working the X10.

Lacking both a destination board and fleet name is this Plaxton Primo at Teesport. YN55 YSC was the second of its type to enter production. New to TM Travel in 2006, she was photographed on contract work at Teesport, in the ownership of M & D Travel.

New to West Yorkshire PTE in 1984 this Leyland Olympian/Roe combination was photographed at Belasis Avenue, Billingham, in June 2020. I was unable to ascertain the ownership of the bus, although it was still taxed. Note the tough-looking Ford F100 imported from the USA.

At Hylton Red House, Stagecoach No. 28004 proudly proclaims 'Check out our new ride – it's a gas'. She is working service 16 between Hastings Hill and Hylton Red House, or 'Red House' as it is known locally.

The tower of St Mary's Roman Catholic Church, Stockton-on-Tees, dominates this picture of Go North East No. 6309. She is working the Sunday variant of the X10 to Peterlee and Newcastle. St Mary's (1841–42) was designed by Augustus Pugin, although the tower was not completed until around 1908, well after his death in 1852.

Diamond-branded Go North East No. 5443 prepares to tackle road works at Front Street, Edmondsley, in July 2020. Charming countryside interspersed with former colliery villages predominate in this hilly corner of County Durham.

Engine trouble for an unidentified Arriva Alexander Dennis Enviro400 at Marina Way, Hartlepool. This was once the site of the timber yard at Jackson Dock. The whole area, including the former United bus depot, was redeveloped by the Teesside Development Corporation in the 1990s.

Arriva No. 1484 leaves Ryde Road, Roseworth, bound for Thornaby on American Independence Day 2020. As all good students know, the thirteen colonies declared independence from Great Britain on 4 July 1776.

The A66 passes right through the heart of central Middlesbrough via a flyover seen on the right of the photograph. Arriva No. 1454 passes along Wilson Street on the frequent service to Netherfields during July 2020.

An impending storm threatens traffic at the approach to the Billingham Beck Branch Bridge and Tees (Newport) Bridge at Portrack. Stagecoach No. 36084 is closest to the camera in this July 2020 picture.

Arriva's training fleet at Stockton-on-Tees can often be spotted around Teesside with new recruits at the wheel. Photographed during a brutal storm from left to right are No. 9992 (DAF SB3000), No. 9994 (Volvo B10BLE) and No. 9996 (VDL SB200). Taken in July 2020.

Thornaby is a proudly independent town situated between Stockton-on-Tees and Middlesbrough. Arriva No. 1486 resplendent in Frequenta branding was photographed on Westbury Street, Thornaby, during July 2020.

A grab shot at North Ormesby showing Arriva No. 1759. The bus is a Transbus Dart SLF/ Transbus Mini Pointer. My brain is not able to process all the name changes this basic design has had over the years. The orange livery was for a now terminated Sainsbury's contract at Whitby. Taken on 6 July 2020.

Two Arriva North East buses collect passengers at North Ormesby in July 2020. Nearest to the camera is No.1534, a VDL SB200/Plaxton Centro. At the rear is No. 1552, a Sapphire-branded Wright Streetlite DF/Streetlite Max Micro-Hybrid new in 2014. North Ormesby is situated to the east of Middlesbrough town centre and has an atmosphere reminiscent of East London.

One of the many large estates on Sunderland's north side is Hylton Castle. Named after the ruined castle constructed by William de Hylton (1376–1435), the structure sits beside Washington Road. At Cheadle Road, a Fiat Ducato, operated by Gateshead Central Taxis, and a Stagecoach Enviro collect customers on a busy Thursday morning.

Close to Sunderland's boundary with Boldon is this elegant Dennis Dart SLF. Stagecoach No. 35189 is setting out to Doxford Park at Kingsway Road, Downhill.

In Dots branding, Stagecoach No. 27245 has just crossed Lustrum Beck at Norton Bridge. She is photographed approaching Stockton-on-Tees working service 35. In Cleveland Transit days the service was usually operated by Fleetlines, Bristol VRs or Dennis Dominators – buses with far more character than modern counterparts.

Representing the new Stagecoach livery at Sunderland is No. 27739. The location is Emsworth Road on the boundary between Carley Hill and Witherwack. Sunderland was granted city status in 1992.

On rising ground above Chester-le-Street is the former colliery community of Grange Villa. At Pelton Lane, Coast & Country-branded No. 5406 prepares to make a tight turn towards Consett. Taken on 8 July 2020.

The mixture of traditional heritage livery on a decidedly modern design makes for a slightly strange juxtaposition/sight. Northern-branded No. 8319, complete with dashcam, was photographed working towards Chester-le-Street in the village of West Pelton.

The remote village of Allenheads, Northumberland, is further south than Gateshead and Sunderland. Ideal for remote routes with low population densities is this Go North East Solo No. 671.

Wrekenton is situated on high ground close to the *Angel of the North*. The name Wrekenton is derived from the Roman road Wrekendyke. Quaylink No. 8239, Red Arrows No. 6051 and Fab Fifty Six No. 6090 are photographed at the blustery High Street in July 2020.

The sleek lines of the Mercedes-Benz Citaro are clearly illustrated in this photograph of Go North East's No. 5298 at Newbrough. The Stanegate, a former Roman road, passes through this pretty village, which is situated south of Hadrian's Wall.

Although branded for the X46 service, Arriva No. 7419 is actually working a local service from Durham to New Brancepeth via Ushaw Moor. The location is New Brancepeth, which is situated above the Deerness Valley.

Despite being in an area once dominated by heavy industry, Newbottle preserves a village green and some notable buildings. Red Arrows-branded No. 6006 works Go North East service X1 towards Easington Lane in 2020.

Go North East's Angel-branded buses provide comfort and refinement for passengers on the Great North Road route. No. 6324 cautiously approaches Front Street, Chester-le-Street, just before lockdown. The town's Methodist church, opened in 1902, can be seen in the background.

This Go North East Optare Solo, No. 720, is ideally suited to negotiating the narrow main road at Quaking Houses. Close to Quaking Houses are the quaintly named settlements of Blackhorse, Maiden Law, The Middles, New Kyo and No Place.

The village of Springwell is home to the Bowes Railway Centre. The railway was first opened in 1826 to serve local collieries and expanded thereafter. Go North East No. 6054 works through the village bound for Newcastle-upon-Tyne.

Spennymoor lost its municipal independence in 1974 with the creation of Sedgefield District Council (later Borough). The Town Hall dwarfs Arriva No. 1474 as she works service 8 in July 2020. County Durham was made a unitary authority on 1 April 2009.

The Whickham View terminus at Denton Burn is a good place to see buses in suburban Newcastle. Stagecoach No. 12062 departs empty for Freeman Hospital via the city centre in July 2020.

St Cuthbert's Church, Blaydon, towers over Go North East No. 3995. She is leaving the bus station bound for Low Prudhoe, Northumberland. Blaydon forms part of the borough of Gateshead and is also a parliamentary constituency.

Stagecoach No. 19670 brightens up a cloudy July day at Lemington. The area was once dominated by the mighty Stella power stations: Stella North at Lemington and Stella South over the River Tyne at Blaydon.

Bells Coaches are based in the delectable village of Stamfordham. The village has a wide village green with a distinctive butter cross dating from 1735. Bells have a sizable fleet of coaches, including Yutong TC9s (YC18 BKA/YD66 AYA), Temsa Safari (YJ10 DUU) and Volvo B8R/Plaxton Leopard. The depot is located on the B6309, at Stamfordham, where this photograph was taken.

Go North East's Toon Link livery is certainly distinctive and also tricky to photograph. Scania Omnicity No. 5239 was captured on layover at Hexham Bus Station. The new bus station at Hexham opened in 2016 and was the subject of considerable controversy.

Tyne Valley Coaches XSV298 and MIG1791, were photographed in the depot yard at Acomb, Northumberland. Acomb is a former colliery village north of Hexham and close to Chester's Roman Fort.

Working the post-war estates of Newton Aycliffe is this Optare Solo (LJU 914). Operated by Hodgsons of Barnard Castle, she had previously operated with Hutchinson of Buckley and P&O Lloyd of Whelston, Flintshire, as MX58 ACO.

Whitley Bay is situated on a glorious stretch of coastline in North Tyneside. The resort was traditionally popular with Scottish holidaymakers and day trippers from the North East. Go North East No. 6105 collects a lone passenger on service 309 to Newcastle at the Links.

Tynedale-branded Solo No. 723 looks out of place in industrial Swalwell. Close to Swalwell are the historic Derwenthaugh Staithes, Axwell Park, plus the affluent community of Whickham.

Go North East No. 6075 negotiates a complex roundabout and heavy traffic as it approaches Blaydon town centre. After calling at the bus station the Volvo B9TL will proceed to Low Prudhoe, gradually leaving behind Tyneside's urban sprawl. Taken in July 2020.

A highly successful bus across Europe is the Mercedes-Benz Citaro. If only AEC, Bristol and Leyland had survived to challenge these fine German products. Go North East No. 5301 was photographed passing through Heddon-on-the-Wall with a typically unclear route number.

At remote Cowshill, a Weardale Mercedes-Benz Sprinter prepares to depart for Stanhope – bereft of any passengers. Cowshill is situated close to the boundary with Cumbria and Northumberland in an area once famous for lead mining.

Entering the stone-built village of Kirk Merrington is Optare Solo MK59 CWU. New to Plymouth Citybus, she is seen at work with Scarlet Band on service 99 to Shildon.

In pouring rain Arriva No. 7493 traverses Maude Terrace at St Helen Auckland. The bus was new to Arriva London in July 2002. St Helen Auckland was previously in the Wear Valley District and is situated between Bishop Auckland and West Auckland.

Heavy traffic makes it hard going for the driver of Go North East's X21 service to Newcastle. No. 6333 was photographed near Westerton in July 2020.

It was a day of sunshine and showers in County Durham on 10 July 2020. Climbing up Dale Road, Shildon, is Arriva No. 7536, bound for Darlington via Heighington. Shildon is a town famous for its railway heritage, including the remains of Soho Engine Works, Hackworth House and the Shildon Tunnel, which opened in 1842. The railway works sadly closed in 1984.

Sea Crest Road, Newbiggin-by-the-Sea, is the location of this elderly Volvo B7TL. Numbered 7486 in the Arriva fleet, she was new in 2001 to Arriva London and is based at Ashington.

There is no mistaking the name of this company at Stanhope. Lined up from left to right are YJ59 GGA (Optare Solo), SK06 AHG (Scania Omnicity) and X6 WMS (Dennis Trident/Plaxton).

The Volvo B10M was a highly successful and reliable chassis that comprehensively outsold rivals such as the Leyland Tiger. New in 1986, this Plaxton Paramount-bodied example was photographed in fine order at Stanhope depot.

A striking machine at Stanhope depot is 6 WMS, a Van Hool Astromega TDX integral. A coach with immense presence, she would be tricky to drive in Upper Weardale but a breeze on the straight roads of the A1M.

A busy scene at Middridge. Arriva No. 1406 passes Arriva No. 1590 at South Side. In the far distance, towards Shildon, is Arriva No. 1605. Middridge is located between Newton Aycliffe and Shildon.

Located just within the North York Moors National Park is the village of Easington. Arriva No. 1451 reaches the end of it journey from Middlesbrough at Grinkle Lane in July 2020. Nearby Loftus depot closed in 2009.

Approaching Cruddas Park, Newcastle, on route 1 to Slatyford is Stagecoach No. 19674. Cruddas Park has a number of high-rise flats that form a distinctive cluster near Westmorland Road. The towers also appear in the opening credits of the classic BBC series *Whatever Happened to the Likely Lads?* (1973–74).

Coatham Coaches have a large fleet of vehicles at their Margrove Park depot near Guisborough. Six examples from the well-maintained fleet are seen at Margrove Park on 11 July 2020.

Go North East have a sizeable number of Ford Transit Connect vans for staff duties. These neat little vehicles can be seen around the network. Closest to the camera at the rear of Percy Main depot is No. 1055 with No. 1044 behind.

The bright orange Fab Fifty Six livery is difficult to miss. No. 6096 brightens up a slightly foreboding sky at Vermont, Washington, in July 2020.

One of the more unexpected buses to work service 56 was this open-top Volvo B7TL/Plaxton President combination. Branded for the Toon Tour, No. 3997 was new in 2001 and was based at Percy Main depot when photographed at Southwick.

Westmorland Road, Elswick, is the location of Stagecoach No. 19432, resplendent in advertising for the company's Megabus operation. She is operating a truncated service 1 to Buddle Road, South Benwell. The journey between the fringe of Newcastle city centre and South Benwell is marked by typical inner-city characteristics plus splendid vistas of the River Tyne.

A neat little machine is K16 GLY, a Volvo B9M/Van Hool combination. Operated by Glynns of Seaton Sluice, she was new to Ralph Coaches, Slough, in 1992. With seats for thirty-six passengers, she is perhaps a little over-engineered for today's requirements. Cheaper, if probably less durable, van-derived mini coaches have become more popular in recent years. The location is Seaton Sluice, Northumberland.

Blyth Library forms the backdrop for Arriva No. 1402, a VDL SB200/Wright Commander combination. Having just changed drivers, she will depart for Morpeth via Bedlington Station.

Social distancing was in place as passengers boarded this charming little Alexander-Dennis Dart. New in 2005, No. 1760 is in exemplary condition for her age. The location is Bridge Street, Blyth.

Arriva No. 2816 crosses the railway line at Bedlington South Signal Box at Bedlington Station. The eponymous railway station was opened in 1850 by the Blyth & Tyne Railway. The station, which closed in 1964, is still extant and there are proposals to reopen the Blyth & Tyne in the future, which poses potential competition for PSV operators.

Gateshead Central Taxis operate this slightly aggressive-looking Alexander Dennis E20D in Nexus livery. She is seen outside the Beacon Shopping Centre at North Shields in July 2020. A ferry connects the town with South Shields.

Turning into the village of Woodhorn is Arriva No. 7510. New to Abellio London, LJ56 VTL was acquired from Ensignbus to replace accident-damaged No. 7513. Out of shot is Lynemouth Power Station, which opened in 1972.

West Road and Westgate Road form the boundary between the wards of Wingrove and Elswick within Newcastle. Traversing this cosmopolitan area is newly painted Stagecoach No. 11502. Hadrian's Wall was located here, the Vallum being to the south and Condercum Fort further west.

Arriva's Temsa Avenues are certainly not the most aesthetically pleasing buses. No. 4702 is pursued by an unidentified sister vehicle in central Middlesbrough.

Stagecoach No. 36466 has just passed under the Port Clarence Branch at Haverton Hill. The former Furness Shipyard entrance was to the right and Haverton Hill station was located to the left of the bridge. The metal section of the bridge was forged by Motherwell Bridge Co., Lanarkshire, in 1922.

Photographed on layover at Morpeth is this anonymous-looking Transbus Dart SJ53 AWX, in service with PCL Travel of Prudhoe. The bus has had several owners, including Filers of Ilfracombe, RJ's of Wem and easyCoach (*sic*) of Shrewsbury.

Service 680, between Hexham and Bellingham, was once operated by Tyne Valley Coaches of Acomb. Now the preserve of Go North East, Citaro No. 5303 prepares to cross the River North Tyne at Bellingham.

Howard Snaith Coaches of Otterburn are a familiar sight around the North East. At the depot in Otterburn are a variety of both full-sized and mini coaches. Worthy of note is the Seddon Atkinson wrecker L24 FAJ – Seddon being another defunct British manufacturer.

Passengers wearing face masks cautiously follow social distancing rules as they board Arriva No. 7175, bound for Morpeth. As usual the destination board is difficult to read in bright sunlight. The location is the village of Thropton, July 2020.

The Optare Solo has proven to be a popular and versatile vehicle that can be seen operating in a variety of environments. Glen Valley Tours operate this short-wheelbase version, YJ54 UXH. The Solo is seen at Chatton, working the Wooler to Alnwick service with an inadequate destination board.

Borders Buses No. 11210 is a Mercedes-Benz OC500LE/MCV Evolution. Borders Buses services cover a wide geographical area, including Biggar, Edinburgh, Ford, Galashiels, Hawick, Holy Island, Peebles and Selkirk. No. 11210 departs Wooler on the 464 to Berwick-upon-Tweed.

Stagecoach No. 11282 works the busy West Road, Newcastle, during rush hour, bound for Chapel House. Condercum Roman Fort stood in the vicinity of this photograph. Taken on 28 July 2020.

Bound for Owington Farm, Stagecoach No. 26277 is about to pass over the railway line at Roseberry Bridge, Billingham. Street lighting creates a cluttered backdrop to this August 2020 view.

In absolutely miserable August weather, Arriva Cross Pennine No. 4661 enters the village of Melkridge. Service 685 represents Arriva's remaining presence in deepest Tynedale. Taken on 4 August 2020.

Haltwhistle claims to be the centre of Great Britain, and it probably is, at least while the Union holds. Go North East's Optare Solo No. 635 leaves the attractively restored railway station, bound for Hexham.

Hadrian's Wall was started in AD 122 along the Tyne-Solway isthmus. Most of the wall was constructed from stone, although a significant stretch was turf wall. A Go North East Optare Solo, with few tourists, works service AD 122. No. 635 was photographed near Carvoran, above Greenhead.

A magnificent-looking beast is this tri-axle Neoplan Tourliner OY67 DXT. Even in plain white, she is an impressive-looking machine. The location is picturesque Chollerford, Northumberland.

Resting at Norton Road, Norton, is Stagecoach No. 27250. Taken in August 2020.

Stagecoach No. 22412 had just endured a complex series of roadworks between Westerhope and North Walbottle when pictured in August 2020. New in 2006, MAN 18.220/Alexander was photographed at North Walbottle.

There is no mistaking the name of this road in Hartlepool – Station Approach. Arriva No. 1320, a Dennis Dart SLF4/Alexander Enviro200, enters Church Street bound for Durham. The area around Church Street and Lynn Street forms the original commercial area of West Hartlepool. Taken in August 2020.

An ungainly lighting column mars the view of Go North East's No. 5202. Now in the training fleet, she was caught at rest at Park Lane, Sunderland, before the mid-August heatwave.